# Vajrayogini Sadhana and Commentary

Published in commemoration of the 2550th Mahaparinirvana anniversary of Buddha Shakyamuni

Vajrayogini Sadhana and Commentary

By
Geshe Ngawang Dhargyey
Summer, 1982
Seattle, Washington

Translated by
Alan Wallace

To be read only by those persons who have received the initiation of Vajrayogini

LIBRARY OF TIBETAN WORKS AND ARCHIVES

© 1992 Library of Tibetan Works & Archives

Revised Edition: 2006

ALL RIGHTS RESERVED

No part of this publication may be reproduced, stored in a retrieval system, or transmitted in any form or by any means, electronic, mechanical, photocopying, recording or otherwise, without the prior permission of the bearer of copyright.

ISBN: 81-86470-54-9

Published by the Library of Tibetan Works and Archives, Dharamsala, and printed at Indraprastha Press (CBT), 4 Bahadur Shah Zafar Marg, New Delhi-110002.

Content

Foreword	vii
Short Vajrayogini Sadhana Commentary	
Introduction	1
Yoga of Sleep	1
Yoga of Rising	2
Yoga of Tasting the Nectar	2
Yoga of Immeasurables	3
Refuge	4
Raking the three bodies as the path	5
Cultivation of the awakening mind	6
Guru Yoga	7
Yoga of Self generation	8
Yoga of Donning the Armour	11
Yoga of Purifying the Sentient Beings	13
Yoga of Blessing the Dakas and Dakinis	13
Yoga of Verbal and Mental Recitation	16
First tangential practice to the completion stage	18
Second tangential practice to the completion stage	20
Inconceivable Yoga	22
Yoga of Daily Activities	24
Tsok Offering	25
Retreat	28
Appendix1 Short Vajrayogini Sadhana	43
Appendix 2 Vajrayogini Prayer	47
Notes 49	
Bibliography	51

Foreword

The Library of Tibetan Works & Archives is pleased to be able to publish Vajrayogini Sadhana and Commentary, a translation of an oral explanation given by Geshe Ngawang Dhargey in Seattle, Washington, U.S.A., in 1981. Traditionally, the practice of tantra is supposed to be kept secret, and it is to be noted that this book is intended purely for those who have received the proper initiations. However, as His Holiness the Dalai Lama has advised, the great misunderstandings to which tantra is often subject to are more harmful than the partial lifting of such secrecy, so there is a necessity for books to be made available which contain authentic explanations.

LTWA is deeply grateful to Gen Rinpoche Geshe Ngawang Dhargey for giving the permission to publish this text. We would also like to acknowledge the fine translation by Alan Wallace and Richard Guard's final editing.

Sale and Distribution of this book is restricted. It is requested that only those with Highest Yoga Tantra initiation, preferably that of Vajrayogini, should read this book. Responsibility for this lies entirely with the reader and according to tradition, disregarding this could have detrimental results.

We hope that this book will be of benefit to those serious students interested in practising the Vajra Path to enlightenment for the welfare of all sentient beings.

Gyatsho Tsering
Director, LTWA

December 1992

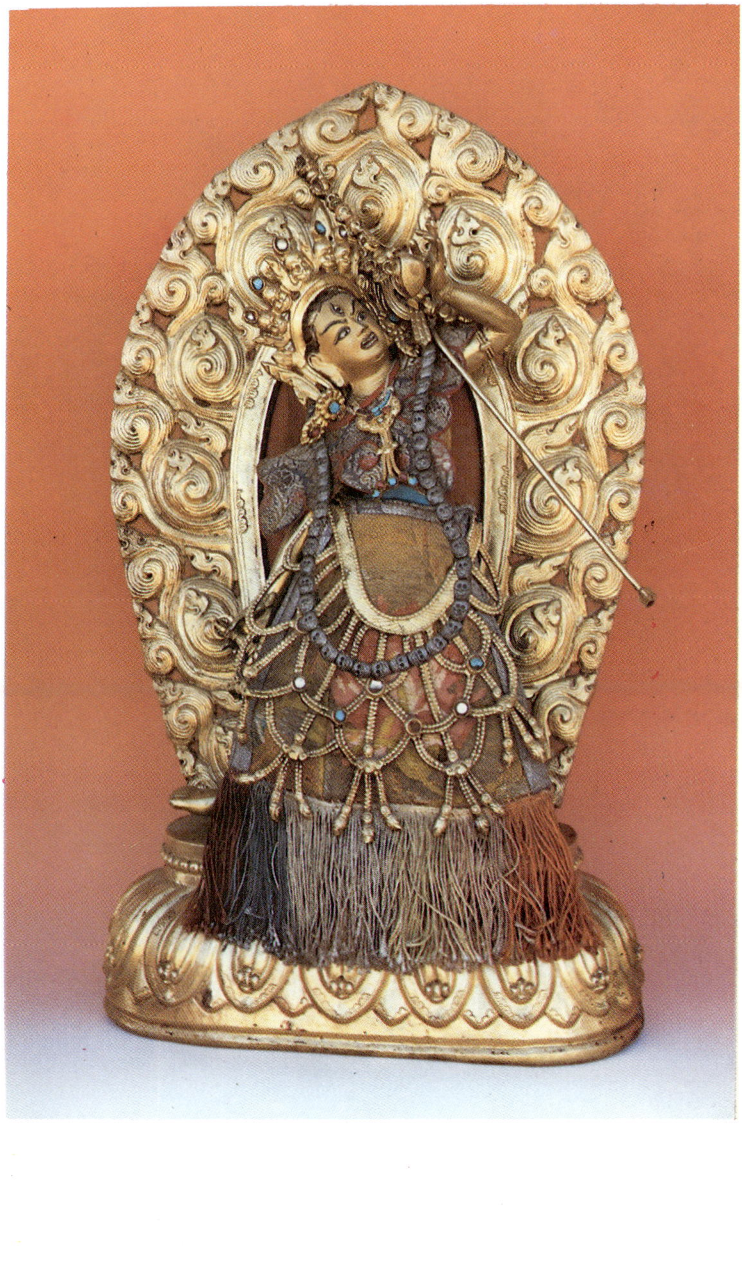

Introduction

We should begin cultivating the awakening mind, aspiring for the highest enligthenment for the sake of all creatures throughout space, and then listen to this teaching with such a motivation towards that goal. There is no more profound teaching than this, for it includes the lineage of the oral transmission from Vajrayogini which she gave directly to Naropa in a vision, and also includes the Naro Khacho oral lineage held by the Sakyapas. This is one of their Golden Dharmas which they retained with great secrecy for a very long time. It is also said that Vajrayogini was Je Tsongkhapa's innermost yidam, kept very secret to his heart.

I will explain this very brief sadhana or self-generation of Vajrayogini. It is comprised of eleven yogas.

Yoga of Sleep

This first of these is the 'yoga of sleep'. In order to practise this, as you lie down to sleep at night, generate yourself as Vajrayogini with one face and two arms, inside the double tetrahedral mandala. When you lie down, place your head in Guru Vajradharma's lap. Unlike Vira Vajradharma, who holds a damaru and skull-cap and supports a khatvamga, Guru Vajradharma holds a vajra in his right hand and a bell in his left. You imagine placing your head in his lap. If you go to sleep like this, then your sleep is extremely wholesome and virtuous. In contrast, if you go to sleep with the mind dominated by attachment, anger or confusion, your entire sleep becomes non-virtuous.

Yoga of Rising

The next yoga is the 'yoga of rising'. Upon awakening, you should imagine being roused by the sound of damarus and by the mantra of Vajrayogini, which is called the 'three OM' mantra. The mantra is being spoken and the damarus sounded by the dakinis of the three abodes,[1] and the sound is coming from the clear light. Then, as you get out of bed, you should do so while continuing to generate yourself as Vajrayogini. As you wash your face and so on in the morning, imagine that you are washing your face as Vajrayogini. As you dress, you are putting on your clothes as Vajrayogini. Every activity you do at the start of the day should be done with this mindfulness of yourself as Vajrayogini. In each case you are offering the bathing, offering the clothes and so forth to Vajrayogini, so that these activities become virtuous.

Yoga of Tasting the Nectar

The third yoga is the 'yoga of tasting the nectar'. This is very straightforward. The nectar should be in some type of vessel. It could be a cup, but definitely one that has a lid. What you are experiencing is called the inner offering (*nang mchod*). The actual substance can be either alcohol or tea, into which you dissolve a blessed nectar pill which has been blessed by a qualified lama. Place the cup or vessel of inner offering into the palm of your right hand, and with your left ring finger draw the three points of a triangle symbolizing the tetrahedral reality source while reciting OM AH HUM. While saying OM, touch the base of your palm, saying AH, touch the right and with HUM the left side. Then dip your finger into the centre of the vessel and thinking that you are taking the essence of the inner offering, place a drop on your tongue and taste it, while imagining that you are experiencing great bliss indivisible with emptiness. The OM AH HUM is an extremely profound mantra, and has an especially great blessing.

Yoga of the Immeasurables

Next is the 'yoga of immeasurables'. This yoga includes not only the four immeasurables, but also taking refuge and cultivating the awakening mind.

First of all you should imagine in the space before you an four-petalled multi-coloured lotus seat, and in the centre of this is your root lama in the form of Cakrasamvara, blue in colour. Cakrasamvara is in the very centre of the lotus, and in front of him, on the lotus petal closest to you, is Vajrayogini, red in colour. All the meditational deities (Yidam) surround Vajrayogini. Surrounding Cakrasamvara on the central part of the lotus, are all the lamas of the guru lineage of vajra yogini, as well as all of one's own gurus, including those lamas from whom one has not received the initiation or transmission of the teachings of Vajrayogini. They form a circle surrounding Cakrasamvara. In an even larger circle surrounding the entire lotus outside the outer edges of the petals are Dharma protectors. The one closest to you is Tent Mahakala, and in the same circle of protectors is Four-armed Mahakala and the Lord and Lady of the Charnel Grounds (all of which are associated with Vajrayogini and Cakrasamvara).

To the right of Cakrasamvara (your left) is Buddha Shakyamuni, who is surrounded by all the Buddhas of the sutra vehicle. Behind Cakrasamvara is a mountain of the Cakrasamvara tantras, including the root tantra called the *Lesser Samvara Tantra*, the explanatory *Samvarodaya Tantra*, and the *Arisal of Heruka*. These appear as scriptures, but you should understand them as visible manifestations of Buddha's wisdom. To Cakrasamvara's left (your right) is Manjushri surrounded by all the dakas and dakinis, bodhisattvas, solitary realizers, and hearers (i.e. the Sangha of the three vehicles).

Holding this visualization directly before you, you are sitting in the centre, and to your right is your own father and a vast host of all the male sentient beings. To your left is your own mother and all the female sentient beings. Directly in front of you, with everyone facing forward, are your enemies, and then the malignant spirits and miscellaneous adversaries. 'Miscellaneous adversaries' refers to people whom you haven't directly harmed. In fact you don't have a bad relationship with them at all, but through some apparent mischance they are causing harm to you. For example, if someone living in your house were murderer, unbeknownst to you, and some other people came to your house to take revenge, and started beating you because you were giving shelter to this person, this would be a case of a 'miscellaneous adversary'. They are in front of you, and behind you are your students, friends and so forth. All of these people are facing forward and looking up to the objects of refuge. As you recite the verses of refuge, you take the role of a chanting leader, so that as you recite, you imagine all the sentient beings around you joining in with this taking of refuge.

Now, to cultivate the causes for taking refuge, first of all you cultivate fear and anxiety, not only for yourself, but for all creatures trapped within the sufferings of the cycle of existence, and specifically fear and anxiety about the dangers of the lower states of birth. Then, looking toward the objects of refuge, you cultivate the conviction that apart from the Guru and the Triple Gem there is no other refuge that can provide a path to free you from this suffering. In this way, you cultivate a very strong conviction and faith in the objects of refuge. It is often said that there are two causes of taking refuge: fear of cyclic existence and the lower states of birth, and faith in the objects of refuge. For the uncommon Mahayana refuge, however, there is a third cause of taking refuge, which is a great yearning for all beings to be enligtthened.

Refuge

Now we come to the sadhana itself. 'I and all living beings as extensive as space, from this time forth until the attainment of the essence of enligthenment, go for refuge to the glorious sacred Gurus.' When cultivating this aspect of refuge, you focus particularly on the central figure of Chakrasamvara and the spiritual masters surrounding him. For the next line of refuge, 'We go for refuge to the fully enligthened Bhagavan Buddhas,' you focus especially on the Buddha Shakyamuni and the Buddhas of the sutra vehicle surrounding him, and on Vajrayogini and the Buddhas of the tantric vehicle surrounding her. Next, 'We go for refuge to the sacred Dharma teachings.' For this aspect of refuge, you concentrate on the volumes of scripture behind Chakrasamvara. Next, 'We go for refuge to the Sangha community of Arya noble ones.' At this point you mainly focus on Manjushri and on the dakas and dakinis surrounding him, as well as on the protectors surrounding all. These verses of refuge are to be recited three times.

Going to the next line, 'I prostrate to and take refuge in the Gurus and the three Precious Gems, and request you to bless my mind stream with waves of inspiring strength.' 'You' is in the plural: all of you, please bless my mind. Having made this request, you imagine that innumerable rays of white light from Buddha Shakyamuni and the Buddha refuges mentioned above come and strike the point between your eyebrows. This is in order to request the Buddha refuge for their blessings. When you request the blessing of the Dharma refuge aspects of the visualisation, the blessings come from the texts, representing the Buddha's wisdom, in the form of rays of red light which merge and dissolve at your throat. Then, to receive the blessings of the Sangha refuge, you imagine that rays of dark blue light come from Manjushri and the rest of the Sangha aspect of the visualisation. These rays of blue light strike and dissolve at your heart. At the conclusion of this visualisation, you should have the conviction that you have received the blessings of the Buddhas, Dharma and Sangha.

Taking the Three Bodies as the Path

Having received the blessings, you should do a very abbreviated meditation of taking the three Bodies of the Buddha as the path. The first aspect of this is that your own body of flesh and bone dissolves. Here you should cultivate the confidence of being the

Truth Body of Vajrayogini, specifically the truth Body of Vajrayogini that you will become on attaining complete enligthenment. You identify with this Truth Body. There are three aspects to this practice up to this point in the meditation: what is perceived is an absence of any appearance, what is ascertained is the lack of inherent existence of all phenomena, and what is experienced is the wisdom of great bliss. With these three aspects, you cultivate the confidence of identifying with the Truth Body of Vajrayogini, which you will become on attaining complete enligthenment. While maintaining this confidence, you should consider that 'if I simply remained as the Truth Body, I would be invisible to everyone except other Buddhas. In that case I wouldn't be of much help.' Therefore, you cultivate the intention of arising as an Enjoyment Body. With this motivation, there suddenly arises from this empty nature of the Truth Body an eight-petalled lotus, and in its centre is a pillar of red light about one cubit high. This arises spontaneously, like a fish leaping out of still water, or a cloud appearing in a clear sky. With this arisal of a one-cubit high pillar of red light, you identify strongly with the Enjoyment Body of Vajrayogini that you will become when you attain enligthenment. Having this pride in being the Enjoyment Body, you should further reflect that 'as long as I remain in the Enjoyment Body form, I will be inaccessible to anyone who has not attained at least the first Bodhisattva ground.' Therefore, in order to become accessible and of benefit to a greater number of beings, you arouse the intention to manifest yourself as an Emanation Body, a grosser form than the Enjoyment Body. Then instantaneously the red pillar of light transforms into yourself as Vajrayogini with one face and two arms. This is the Emanation Body form of yourself as Vajrayogini. You attain enlightenment as Vajrayogini. This vision appears, and you identify with this Vajrayogini.

Cultivation of the Awakening Mind

In this short sadhana, there is no inner offering, so we proceed directly to the line for cultivating the awakening mind. For the line which states 'Once I have attained the state of a fully enligthened Buddha', the point of doing so is to free all sentient beings from the ocean of suffering of cyclic existence. In order to accomplish this, I shall practise the stages of Vajrayogini's path. This concludes the fourth yoga, the yoga of the immeasurables.

Guru Yoga

The fifth yoga is called the 'guru yoga'. This is found in the context of the sutras as well as in the tantric part of Buddhist practice. The Guru is the root of all common and supreme attainments, and especially in the context of the highest yoga tantra, the Gurus are of the utmost importance. You should not regard the Guru as merely an ordinary Guru, but as Vajradharma, and not only is the Guru himself Vajradharma, but even each pore of his body is also Vajradharma.

To begin this Guru yoga, do the following visualisation in the space before you, specifically at the level of the point between your eyebrows. If it is higher it leads to agitation, and if lower it leads to sluggishness and sinking. So at the level of the eyebrows, you visualise a throne made of jewels and supported by eight lions. Upon that jewel throne is a lotus seat, and upon that is a moon disc. Seated on this seat of lotus and moon is your own root Guru from whom you have received the initiation and the oral transmission of Vajrayogini. He is the aspect of Vira Vajradharma, and is about the distance of one full prostration in front of you. Vajradharma is in the form of a sixteen-year-old youth, red in colour. With his right hand he is playing emptiness. With his left hand, he holds at his heart a skull-cup filled with nectar. With his left shoulder he supports a khatvanga, which is a type of staff with a vajra at its upper tip. His two legs are crossed in the vajra position. He is adorned with the six bone ornaments, as commonly seen in tantric practice. These are the crown, earrings, necklace, bracelets and anklets, making five, and human ash smeared over the body, which is the sixth. You should look on Guru Vajradharma as being the embodiment of all objects of refuge: all combined into this one form. If you were to do this elaborately, you would visualise more than the central figure, but for us this might be too cumbersome. Doing it the elaborate way, which is not necessary, you would have to visualise all of the thirty-eight Guru of this Vajrayogini lineage. You do not have to do it so elaborately. Simply focus on this one form of Vajradharma, and imagine him to be the embodiment of all the objects of refuge.

Now you recite the verse. First of all, 'I make request to you, precious Guru, who are the essence of all the Buddhas of the three times' means that I prostrate and take refuge in the precious Guru, who is the nature of all the Buddhas of three times. 'I request you to bless my mindstream with waves of inspiring strength' means that you request the Guru to bless your mind which is dominated by self-grasping, and to make your mind more wholesome and receptive for the rest of the blessing.

This is recited three times, after which the Lama dissolves into red light and comes to the crown of your head. Purely out of compassion for you, he dissolves and comes to you in this way, and then with great affection and compassion he enters through the crown and dissolves down into your body, arriving at the heart. At the heart he transform into the aspect of a red syllable BAM. You should imagine at this point that the Guru's mind and your mind have become inseparable, indivisible. This is in fact what occurs: your own mind and the Guru's mind stream do become indivisible on your attainment of complete enligthenment. This concludes the Guru yoga, the fifth of the eleven yogas.

Yoga of Self-generation

For the sixth yoga, the 'yoga of self-generation', first visualise at your heart the two syllables E-E (ཨེ་ཨེ་). These two syllables face each other. Although in most cases seed syllables face each other.

Although in most cases seed syllables are visualised upright, in this case these are lying down end-to-end so that the *dreng bu* (E-sound) vowels on top of each letter are together, and the rest of the two syllables are coming out like two wings. They look like two people lying down with their heads together. These two E's transform into a double tetrahedron. This is like two pyramids intertwined, with the three corners of one rotated forty-five degrees from the other, so that the combined figure has six equidistant points on the horizontal plane. The two pyramids point downward, so that their lower points converge into one, and their bases form a horizontal surface on top. In the centre of this is a syllable AH, which transforms into a white moon disc. At the centre of the moon disc is a red syllable BAM, standing upright. The red BAM syllable at the centre of the moon disc is surrounded by the letters of the mantra OM OM SARVA BUDDHA DAKINIYE VAJRA VARNANIYE VAJRA VAIROCHANIYE HUM HUM HUM PHAT PHAT PHAT SVAHA, which are also standing upright. These syllables are arranged counterclockwise. Now from the BAM syllable and the letters of the mantra radiate rays of red light which completely fill your entire body, purifying the disorders, evil spirits, unwholesome imprints and obscureness of your body, speech and mind. Now your body itself transforms into an egg-shaped mound of red light, which transforms into yourself as Vajrayogini.

Now you are appearing as Vajrayogini, and she is standing on a seat made of horizontal sun disc which rests on a multi-coloured lotus. Her right leg is extended, and her foot is pressing on the breasts of red Kalarati (*Dus mtsan dmar mo*), who is Ishvara's consort. Pressing on her breasts symbolizes conquering attachment or lust. Her left leg is slightly bent, with her foot resting on the back of the head of black Ishvara (*'Jigs byed nag po*), the back of the head being the location of the arisal of anger. She is red in colour and has a splendour like that of the universe-destroying fire at the end of an eon. She has one face, two arms and three eyes. She gazes upward at the pure land of Kechari, symbolizing on the one hand that she has herself attained this pure land, and on the other hand that for those who open themselves to her, she will lead them to this pure land. In her outstretched right hand she is holding a clever, which is marked with a vajra and faces downwards. In her left hand she holds aloft a skull-cup filled with blood. A little bit of the blood in the skull-cup is overflowing, dripping down into her mouth. Resting on her left shoulder is a khatvanga marked with a vajra. This is a hidden manifestation of the deity Heruka. She has jet black hair, not tied up in knots and so forth, but flowing freely down to her waist. She is very youthful in form. She has very full, upright breasts, with an appearance that can produce the highest form of happiness, which is great bliss. You should think of these as being able to produce the great joy of wisdom of inseparable bliss and emptiness. As a head ornament she is wearing a crown of five dried human heads, and around her neck is a long necklace of fifty dried human heads, symbolising the purification of the impure fifty-one mental factors. She adorned with the five ornaments. She, the consort, has only five whereas the male deity has six. She does not have the human ash, which symbolizes white bodhicitta. She is standing in the midst of a great mass of wisdom fire, whirling counterclockwise. This is the fire of the wisdom which burns away all the obstacles to liberation and to full enligthenment.

If I were teaching this in the ancient tradition, there would be three teachings on this subject: an elaborate teaching, an intermediate teaching and a concise teaching. Then the following day, each day's teaching would be reviewed. However, due to lack of time, this presentation will have to suffice. The traditional method is following the practice of the Sakya lineage, which is the tradition of this deity practised by the junior tutor to His Holiness Kyabje Trijang Rinpoche. On the many occasions when I received this teaching from Kyabje Trijang Dorjechang, I found that what I was actually receiving were what is called experiential instructions, where the lama is teaching from his own experience. In such a case, the disciples are following the same meditation and striving for the same experience that the Guru has already achieved. Now I am giving this teaching, and I urge you all to begin practicing.

You should truly rejoice in the opportunity to follow such a meditation, for one has to have accumulated very extraordinary karma in order to receive the initiation required to study and practise these teachings. You should recognise this and engage in the practice with great delight.

Now, returning to the sadhana, Vajrayogini abides in the midst of blazing wisdom fire. This concludes the yoga of self-generation.

Yoga of Donning the Armour

Next is the 'yoga of donning the armour'. In this practice, you visualise very small moon disc between the skin and the flesh. The first one is at the navel, and upon it are the two red syllables OM and BAM. These are standing upright on the moon disc. Red light emanates from these syllables, creating a broad belt of red light around one's entire abdomen from the navel up to the heart. These syllables are standing upright on the moon disc, and are in the nature of Vajravarahi. At the heart is another white moon disc, upon which are standing the two blue syllables HAM and YAM, which are in the nature of Yamani. From these two syllables at the heart, a band of blue light radiates out around your body from the level of the heart up to the throat. Now at the throat (although the text says 'mouth') there is another moon disc, with the two letters HRIM and MOM. These syllables are white, and are in the nature of Mohani. White light radiates from the two syllables HRIM and MOM at the throat, and this white light goes from the throat up to just above eyebrows. At the forehead there is another moon disc, and upon this are two yellow syllables HRIM HRIM. These are of the nature of Sachalani. Yellow light radiates from these two syllables, forming a band of light from the forehead upward, covering all of the head except the area at the top that would be covered if one were wearing a little skullcap. This is all covered with yellow light. It is very important in the visualisation to cover the body in this way, because 'armour' is not merely a name. It actually does protect you from harmful influences. At the very crown of the head is another moon disc, and upon this are the two green syllables HUM HUM. These are of the nature of the goddess Samtrasani, and they emit a cap of green light. At the joints of each of your limbs are white moon disc, upon which are the syllables PHAT PHAT. These are a smoky-brown colour, and are in the nature of Chandika. The text says all of the joints, but this is actually referring to eight joints: the shoulders, elbow, hip joints and knees. So at each of those joints you visualise a white moon disc with the two smoke coloured syllable PHAT PHAT, radiating smoke coloured light. The two PHATs at the shoulder radiate smoke-coloured light down the upper arm to the elbow. The two PHATs at the elbow radiate smoke-coloured light down to the fingertips. The two PHATs on each hip radiate smoke-coloured light down the thigh to the knee. And the two PHATs on each knee radiate smoke-coloured light down to the tips of your toes.

The two syllables in each of these cases are of the nature of the six dakas and six dakinis. The six dakas represent the five Buddha families, plus the Buddha family of Vajradhara. The six dakinis are the six consorts of those six Buddhas. Therefore, these letters are respectively of the nature of these deities and consorts, and it is the protection of these Buddhas that we are invoking here.

This is a very special and very effective kind of armour or protection particular to Cakrasamvara, the father (*yab*) in Vajrayogini practice. It is effective in two ways: on the one hand in warding off or making yourself invulnerable to outer obstacles, that is to say malignant forces, and on the other hand to keep your inner accomplishments or siddhis from dissipating outwards. It is like people of ancient times wearing iron or steel armour to ward off arrows and so forth.

This is a story of a contest between Nyima Lotzawa and Ra Lotzawa, two great tantric masters. They were battling with their miraculous powers, and Nyima Lotzawa sent Vaishravana and his eight ferocious retinue deities to attack Ra Lotzawa. In the meantime, Ra Lotzawa created a vajra fence around himself, and around that a huge conflagration of vajra flames. When Vaishravana and these eight wrathful beings came to attack Ra Lotzawa, they could not even approach him, so they came back to Nyima Lotzawa, and Vaishravana told him, 'We went there, but that fellow Ra Lotzawa created this vajra fence and fire all around himself, and we couldn't touch him, we couldn't even bear to look at it'. This protective armour we are generating here is similar in effectiveness (not in appearance) to the protection that Ra Lotzawa created.

Yoga of Purifying Sentient Beings

The next yoga is the 'yoga of purifying sentient beings'. In this practice, yourself as Vajrayogini emanates red light which completely fills your body, and then, overflowing in its abundance, is unable to remain inside the body and flows out through the pores, radiating boundlessly in all directions. These rays of light touch all sentient beings, purifying them of unwholesome mental imprints and obscurations, and establishing them in the Kechari (Tibetan: kha chö མཁའ་སྤྱོད་) pure land. This is a very powerful yoga.

Yoga of Blessing the Dakas & Dakinis

The next yoga, which is not in the abbreviated sadhana, is the 'yoga of blessing the dakas and dakinis'. In this yoga, you generate what is called the body mandala. There are twenty-four sacred sites of great blessing in this world, and there are twenty-four places on you own body which correspond to these. In order to practise this yoga (for instance, in connection with the long sadhana), you visualize twenty-four dakinis, one for each of these places, in order to bless the channels and winds of your body as being in the nature of Vajrayogini.

There was a lama in Tibet called Phagmo Drub pa, an extremely fine Kha Chö lama. When he told his disciples that he was considering making a pilgrimage to India to make offerings at the sacred sites there, they pleaded with him not to go but to remain in Tibet. In particular, one of his foremost disciples recited a verse beseeching him to remain. The meaning of this verse is 'These twenty-four sacred places are to be found in the temple of your own body. See the dakas and dakinis who abide in your own body, and collect merit from offering to them right here within you. Remain a guru here where you are now'. So Phagmo Drub pa listened to this request, and after considering for a while and deciding that there was meaning in this, he remained in Tibet.

In the life of Milarepa also, he once sang a song about his guru, saying, 'I hold the guru and the complete mandala here in my heart. Therefore, as I eat, I am making offerings to the guru and the yidam at my heart. How fortunate I am!' You can practise just like Milarepa, by visualizing the guru at your heart in the form of the syllable BAM, the syllable which has the nature of the guru and of the union of bliss and emptiness of the guru's mind. Hold this at your heart, and then as you eat, you collect the merit of making food offerings to the guru. In fact you can make this into a fire puja, a fire offering, by visualizing that your mouth becomes the ritual hearth, and your two hands become the ladle and funnel which are used for a fire puja.

At this point you meditate on the body mandala at the heart. This is rather complicated. You visualise a double tetrahedron at your heart. Within that, slightly below its flat upper surface, you visualise a moon disc. This is called the body mandala, because you are transforming your channels and elements into the nature of the Buddha. Upon this moon disc, in its very centre is the principal deity, Vajrayogini. Around her are four goddesses, one at each of the cardinal directions. The goddess on the left is green, the one in the back is red, the one on the right is yellow, and the goddess in the front is white. Then there is circle of eight goddesses. Beyond that is another circle of eight goddesses, another circle of eight beyond that, and a fourth circle of eight beyond that. Thus there are five circles of goddesses surrounding principal Vajrayogini in the centre, one circle of four and four circles of eight goddesses each. In total there are thirty-seven goddesses. All of these goddesses are in the form of Vajrayogini, although they have different names. They are standing, holding cleaver and skull-cup and, except for the group of four goddesses, are very radiant red in colour.

If you are able to, after visualizing the above, you visualise a double tetrahedral mandala in the heart of the principal Vajrayogini who is in the centre of the moon disc in the heart of yourself as Vajrayogini. Within this double tetrahedral mandala is a BAM syllable surrounded by the three OM mantra in the centre of a moon disc. Of course this innermost mandala and moon disc with BAM and mantra is very tiny. If you are presently unable to do this visualisation comfortably, leave out this aspect of the body mandala practice. Instead, simply visualise a moon disc with a syllable BAM surrounded by the mantra in its centre within the heart of yourself as Vajrayogini. The mantra is arranged counterclockwise.

When you say PHEM! you should accompany the verbal action of this mantra with the physical action of the 'blazing' mudra. Hooking your right forefinger over your left forefinger, with the rest of the fingers stretched over your right forefinger, and placing your left big toe on top of your right big toe, with outstretched arms you bring our hands to the ground at your left side, while glancing out of the corner of your eye at your hands as you do so. Then slowly, with arms still outstretched, bring your hands, with forefingers interlocked, above your head, and gracefully make a small circle with your hands three times counterclockwise, three times clockwise, and again three times counterclockwise. Then, with upraised arms and forefingers still interlocked at the level of your brow in front of you, looking upwards say PHEM! quite loudly, and release the mudra. This is the 'blazing' mudra.

While saving PHEM! and doing this mudra, visualise that innumerable rays of light emanated from the red BAM syllable at your heart, and these invite Vajrayogini, surrounded by all the dakas and dakinis of the ten directions (in general), and (in particular) those residing in the twenty-four sacred places and Akanistha pure land where they reside. Also, since in the previous yoga of purifying sentient beings you established all sentient beings in the state of having the attainment and the form of Vajrayogini, at this moment the rays of light from the BAM also invite all sentient beings. You imagine Vajrayogini, the dakas and dakinis and all sentient beings, all in the form of Vajrayogini, coming to you.

Now you recite the four syllables DZA HUM BAM HOH. With Dza, imagine all these beings in the form of Vajrayogini above you. With HUM, they enter through your crown and descend through your central channel to the BAM syllable at your heart. With BAM, they become inseparable with BAM. Then with HOH, you experience the great bliss of this inseparability. Then, while reciting the mantra OM YOGA SHUDDHA SARVA DHARMA YOGA SHUDDHO HAM, do the embracing mudra. The meaning of this mantra is 'all phenomena are of the nature of the yoga of purity, and I myself am also of that pure nature'.

Yoga of Verbal and Mental Recitation

Next is the 'yoga of verbal and mental recitations'. The verbal recitation involves the utterance of the three OM mantra. The visualisation that should be done during the recitation of this mantra is as follows. Rays of light emanate from the BAM syllable and the mantra, radiating in all directions and purifying the unwholesome mental imprints and obscurations of all sentient beings. Imagine that on the tips of these rays of red light are offering goddesses who make offerings to the Buddhas of all ten directions. The Buddhas accept these offerings and consequently experience the wisdom of great bliss. Then all the Buddhas send forth their blessings and powers, appearing in the form of rays of red light. These converge from all directions and touch the BAM syllable at your heart, so that you feel you have received a mighty blessing from all the Buddhas. While doing the above visualisation, you should recite three OM mantra as many times as you have promised, or if you recite more than that, it is fine. As mentioned above this is a very effective mantra. There is no siddhi, common or supreme, which cannot be attained by using this mantra. In fact, this mantra embodies the essence of all the mantras of all Enligthened goddesses. No matter what one is striving for, even mundane goals such as wealth or long life, this mantra is very effective.

The second part of this yoga is called the mental recitation. This involves no verbal activity at all. Sit in a very correct meditation posture. Focus on the BAM syllable at your heart as being of the same nature as your own mind, such that this is your perspective when you are looking from within your heart. You are not looking down at the BAM syllable at your heart. Your mind itself is the BAM letter, so that is where you are looking from.

You may do the mental recitation exactly as just described, or in conjunction with vase breathing. The method for this is as follows. Sitting in the seven-point posture of Vairochana, visualise the central energy channel, the thickness of the straw, running vertically from its upper end slightly above the point halfway between your eye-brows, passing from there up the centre of you forehead to your crown and then down, slightly in front of your spine, all the way to its lower end three or four finger-widths below your navel. It is flexible like a plantain trunk, smooth like the stem of a lily, and straight like a bamboo trunk. Its colour is blue on the outside and red on the inside. Inhale slowly through both nostrils, visualising that the lower energy-winds ascend slightly from your anus. When first doing this practise, the lower winds should be only slightly raised, giving a gentler effect; when you have gained familiarity with the vase breathing practice, you may raise them to your navel. Breathe out, maintaining the slight elevation of the lower energy-winds. Now inhale again and swallow your saliva soundlessly, while visualising that your upper energy-winds descend. Reaching your heart, these upper energy-winds press down on the phenomena-source with BAM in its centre, and the phenomena-source and energy-winds proceed together down to the navel, where they remain, held there by your concentration. Keep your navel close to your spine, and gently close the door of your secret organ. When doing mental recitation without the vase breathing, the recitation is done while visualising the phenomena-source BAM at your heart. When reciting in conjunction with the vase breathing, it is very important that you do this practice at the navel as described, and do not hold the winds at the heart, as this can cause problems. At this point, hold the breath for as long as is comfortable, while focusing on the BAM syllable as being your own mind, keeping this as your vantage point, and looking at each of the letters surrounding you on the moon disc, one after the other observing in turn every letter of the mantra during the retention of one breath. If you cant make it all the way around in one breath, then look at however many you are able to look at in one breath, and then release that breath, draw another breath and hold it, and continue with the circuit of the mantra where you left off. When you have completed three circuits of the mantra, in however many breaths are necessary, you have completed the mental recitation. This is the method of recitation in conjunction with vase breathing, so called because the upper and lower energy winds are contained by your concentration at your navel, just as water is contained in a vase.

First Tangential Practice to the Completion of Stage

A tangential practice to the completion stage is not a central or principal completion stage practice, but is auxiliary to the actual practice of the completion stage. In order to do this first tangential practice, first you do the vase breathing as before. Then, while holding the upper and lower energy winds at your navel, on top of the double tetrahedral mandala at the navel of yourself as Vajrayogini, do the following visualisation from the point of view of yourself as the central BAM syllable. You, the BAM are standing on the moon disc which is in the centre of the double tetrahedral mandala. Surrounding you are the six points of the double tetrahedron. One point is directly in front of you, one directly behind and two on either side, just like a star of David. All of these points are on a horizontal plane slightly above you. There is nothing within the points directly in front of and behind you, but within the four points, two on either side of you, close to the tips, are twirling bliss wheels, pink in colour. To do this practice, first concentrate for a while on these revolving bliss wheels, from the perspective of yourself as the BAM syllable in the centre. It is important also to view the nada of your own mind, the letter BAM, as blazing with fire. The BAM is actually composed of various parts: the head and the other three lines that make up the main letter, the crescent moon on top of the head of the BAM, the circular drop (*bindu*) on top of that, and the three-curved nada on top of the drop. After looking at the twirling bliss wheels, then especially focus on the nada which is spouting flames upward. Flames are shooting up out of the nada like a flame thrower. The point of this is that you are bringing your consciousness up into the flame arising out of the nada. You are now shifting your focus of identification from being the entire BAM letter to being specifically the flame blazing upward at the tip of the BAM.

Whenever consciousness enters, the energy winds naturally accompany it. Consciousness and energy winds always travel together. As you are bringing your consciousness to this flame, you are simultaneously bringing your energy winds there also. The purpose here is to draw the energy winds into the central channel, by placing your mind here through this visualisation. Just as consciousness and energy winds are always together in mediation, the same is true in everyday life. When a person says that he or she as the disease called '*sog lung*', a disorder of energy winds such that they inappropriately enter that person's heart, the mind automatically accompanies the winds to the heart. Therefore this disease has both mental and physical aspects: the person acts crazy, and there are also physical symptoms of illness. Here, the winds and the mind are going together, in this case to the navel.

This is the first tangential practice to the completion stage. By doing this practice and causing the energy winds to enter the central channel at the navel, you are developing the method which is used in developing realisation when you do the actual completion stage later.

Second Tangential Practice to the Completion Stage

In the second tangential practice, you generate yourself as Vajrayogini and visualise the central channel. Inside the central channel at the forehead, slightly higher than the point between the inner ends of the eyebrows, you visualise a white bliss wheel, in the nature of bodhicitta. This is in contrast to the bliss wheels which are visualised during the initiation, at which time the one at the forehead is red and the one at the navel is white. Here it is reversed: the bliss wheel at the forehead is white and the one at the navel is red. Now, the white bliss wheel inside the central channel at the forehead is spinning in a counterclockwise direction. You follow it as it moves gradually downward through the central channel to the navel, where it continues to spin. At the lower tip of the central channel below the navel you visualise another bliss wheel, also spinning counterclockwise. It is red in colour, and has the nature of fire. This wheel rises up through the central channel, gradually ascending to the navel, where it meets and joins with the white bliss wheel. Now both bliss wheels are revolving together at the navel. Gradually the colours of the two mix until there is just a pink colour. This gradually fades, and one is left with just an experience of emptiness. You should imagine that this is the experience of the emptiness of inherent existence of all phenomena.

This process of meditation is closely related to the death process that we will experience. In the actual stage of death, as the life force which sustains our life becomes exhausted it ceases to uphold the white bodhicitta at the upper end of the central channel, so this white bodhicitta descends to the heart. In that process one experiences a vision of whiteness. Then the red bodhicitta which remains during one's life at the navel is no longer held there, and rises to the heart, at which time one experiences a red vision. Then these two come together at the heart. So there is a very important parallel with this practice. The importance of this practice consists in its being a valuable preparation for death. You can get a head start on preparing for your death which is to come. There is no doubt that each of us will experience death, whether in a few years, a long time, or whenever it may come. We don't have to ask anyone else whether our time to die will come or not. And when we are at the point of dying, we will be completely on our own, and our only help, our only refuge at that time will be our own merit. If we haven't accumulated any virtuous merit, then we will be totally isolated, and we will have very great fear. Shantideva said:

> When seized by the messengers of death,
> What benefit will friends and relatives afford?
> My merit alone will protect me then
> But I have never relied on that.

So if you do in fact engage in practice now and accumulate merit, then it is possible to be free of the fear of death, and to be able to, in a very relaxed way, send your consciousness to the Kechari pure land.

There are many people who save money and so forth as security for their old age, so that when they become old they will be certain to have enough food and resources. However, it really is questionable affair whether that person will reach old age. Perhaps she will never make it that far. She might die in middle age. There is no certainty about this. But as far as death is concerned there is complete certainty. And death itself is a very important opportunity for spiritual practice. There are many practices, especially in terms of tantra, to be done at that time. So it is a great loss, it is a terrible shame, if when people are on the verge of death, they are given injections to make them unconscious and go into coma. This is most unfortunate, because they miss out on something that we all need to practise.

This concludes the explanation of the yoga of the verbal and mental recitations.

Inconceivable Yoga

The next yoga is called the 'inconceivable yoga'. Within this yoga there are two practices, the common yoga and the uncommon or extraordinary yoga. The uncommon yoga is one that may only be taught to three people at a time. It is an extremely profound and highly secret practice. It is said to be superior even to the transference of consciousness (*phowa*) practice. One reason for that is that phowa practice can decrease your life span if you engage in it extensively, whereas with the uncommon inconceivable yoga, not only does your life span not decrease, but its results are more profound and achieved more swiftly than with the phowa practice. It is an uncommon means for beings able to go to the Kechari pure land.

A story is told of a minor translator in Tibet named Purang Lo Chung (*pö rang lo chung*). He was engaging in a strict retreat, so that there was not even an entrance to the cave where he was staying, only a little window through which food was passed to him. He had a retreat assistant who came to bring him his food. One day this assistant saw eight girls outside of the cave, and somehow they got inside the cave. When the assistant looked inside later, the girls weren't there, and neither was the meditator! He had simply disappeared. Word of this got out, and some people thought Purang Lo Chung had gone to Akanistha while others thought that the assistant might have killed him and hidden the body somewhere. No one was able to decide what had really happened, and this was a subject of much discussion in that part of Tibet. After some time, some pilgrims came down from Tibet into Nepal to meet a very great master there. This lama was in particular a master of this Vajrayogini tantra, and was in direct contact with Akanistha. He would go there to ask questions and receive advice. This great lama asked the pilgrims, 'What's happening in your neck of the woods?' and they told him that this translator Purang Lo Chung had disappeared, but that no one knew whether he had disappeared or had actually gone to Akanistha. This lama then went to Akanistha and asked, and he was told, yes, he is here. The eight girls (who were one of the sets of eight Vajrayoginis that you visualise in the body mandala) had invited him there. So he had gone there, taking his body. This is the kind of result that can occur through practising the inconceivable yoga.

For the common inconceivable yoga, after generating yourself as vajrayogini, immeasurable rays of light are emanated from the syllable BAM together with its surrounding mantra. These rays of light pervade the universe, reaching the formless realm, the form realm and the desire realm. Now the formless realm melts into blue light and dissolves into the upper portion of your body, from your crown to your throat. Then the form realm melts into the aspect of red light and dissolves into the middle part of your body, from your throat to your heart. Then the desire realm melts into the aspect of white light and dissolves into the lower part of your body, from your heart down to your toes. At this point there is nothing left but you. You have dissolved the entire universe. The formless, form and desire realms have all dissolved into you. Now you yourself dissolve from your crown downward and from your toes upward, until you have completely dissolved into the tetrahedral phenomena source (mandala) at your heart. Then the phenomena source dissolves into the moon disc.

If you have visualised the body mandala, then it is also dissolved at this time. In this case, the moon disc dissolves into the thirty-two Vajrayoginis of the four circles. The thirty-two Vajrayoginis dissolves into the four Vajrayoginis in the four cardinal directions. These four Vajrayoginis dissolve into the principal Vajrayogini in the centre. Now this principal goddess dissolves from the crown and from the toes, dissolving into the phenomena source in her heart. That dissolves into the moon disc. That dissolves into the encircling mantra. That dissolves into the BAM syllable. Now the lower portion of the BAM dissolves into the 'head' of the BAM, that is the horizontal line on its top. Then the head of the BAM dissolves into the crescent moon, which dissolves into the bindu, which dissolves into the nada. The three curves of the nada successively dissolve from the bottom, until only the topmost curve is left. This thin silver gradually fades into the emptiness of the clear light. Now this clear light is all that remains.

It is very good if in conjunction with this meditation, you also maintain mindfulness of the corresponding successive dissolution of the bodily elements: the earth element dissolving into the water element, water dissolving into fire, fire into air, air into consciousness, consciousness dissolving into its successively subtler aspects, and finally the most subtle consciousness dissolving into emptiness.

This concludes the explanation of the common inconceivable yoga, which is the tenth yoga.

Yoga of Daily Activities

The eleventh yoga, the 'yoga of daily activities', involves yourself arising out of emptiness like a cloud suddenly forming in the sky. In the same way, from within emptiness, you appear suddenly in the form of Vajrayogini. This is the first part of the yoga of daily activities. Following this, there are many other aspects in terms of transforming daily life into the path of Vajrayogini. All these practices involve three perceptions. The first is perceiving any and all forms which are seen, be they good or bad, as being the form of Vajrayogini, manifestation of her body. For the second, whatever is heard, whether it is good or bad speech, pleasant or unpleasant sound, is perceived as the speech of Vajrayogini. Third, whatever occurs in your mind, even if good or wholesome thoughts are a rare event for you, nevertheless, every single mental thought or experience is perceived as being of the nature of the wisdom of the non dual bliss and emptiness of Vajrayogini.

Examples of this yoga are included when you are eating or

drinking, you offer your food and drink to the lama-yidam at your heart. Likewise, whenever clothes are put on these are an offering to the lama-yidam. When it is stated that tantra is a means for attaining enligthenment in this very life, it is by means of just such practices as this that enligthenment becomes an actual possibility, because it is in this way that you rapidly accumulate a vast amount of virtuous merit and purify many obstacles and obscurations.

Another example of the very profound way in which a tantric practitioner accumulates the two types of collections, of wisdom and of merit, is in the practice of the tsok offering. The central offering in this ritual is a cone-shaped cake, usually made of tzampa. This is a material offering. On the basis of that, you are accumulating the merit of making a material offering. Then, taking that tsok offering as a basis for transformation, you meditate on the lack of inherent existence of that offering, and at the same time maintain a mind experiencing great bliss. By thus cultivating the realisation of emptiness conjoined with great bliss you generate this offering as a supreme object of offering. Making the offering in this way accumulates the collection of wisdom. By offering the tsok as a material offering, you are accumulating the collection of merit. By using this method, you are simultaneously accumulating the two collections of merit and wisdom in a very effective and profound way.

Tsok Offering

For the actual explanation of the tsok offering, the tsok itself can be something as simple as a little sack of biscuits or cookies. It is also very good to have some alcohol and some meat (even dried meat is fine). If you don't keep alcohol on hand, you can prepare it beforehand by taking some wheat flour, putting some drops of alcohol in the flour and rolling it up into a ball. Then you can keep this in a container, and whenever you offer tsok, just take out a pinch of flour and this will serve as the alcohol offering. You can do this at meal time, when you are having your lunch or dinner. After preparing a little pill of the alcohol in flour, simply recite the verses of the tsok, which are not very long. If this is impractical, you can say OM AH HUM three times, and then say the single verse for offering the tsok. Having offered this, you can eat the pill along with your meal. There is no reason why you should ever be unable to offer. Even if you are spending your whole day travelling on the train or airplane, you will still eat something, so you can make your food into your offering, and offer it and then eat it.

It is very good if you can memorise these eleven yogas of Vajrayogini, so that you have them on the tip of your tongue. If you read Tibetan, Sakya Pandita has written a poem which contains the summarised names of all of these yogas. Being in verse form, it is very easy to memorise.

The eleven yogas are the means for attaining the outer Kechari pure land, and the two tangential practices to the completion stage are the means for attaining the inner Kechari, which is the wisdom of non-dual bliss and emptiness. If you attain the inner Kechari, you don't need to attain the outer Kechari, because if you have the inner wisdom of non-dual bliss and emptiness, then you can go to the outer Kechari whenever you like. But it is very difficult to accomplish. Therefore, for those who have not attained either, one should strive to attain at least the outer Kechari, which is reached by these eleven yogas. The Akanistha pure land is an extremely fine place to be. Having entered that pure land, you hear of no suffering, you see no suffering. Wherever you look there is no trace of suffering. All of the other inhabitants of this pure land are beings who will attain full enligthenment in one life, in one body. Any material thing you need appears spontaneously, without you having to make any effort for it. Also, you come under the direct guidance of Heruka and his consort. They are your gurus in this land. Your life span is as long as space exists. Having entered this pure land, then by means of your miraculous powers, you are able to visit other pure lands, such as Sukhavati or Tushita. As it states in the *Lama Chopa (Guru Puja)*, if I have gained very high realisations, for example the inner Kechari of this wisdom of non-dual bliss and emptiness, then there is no real need to go to the outer Kechari. But if at the point of death I have not gained this, then I must do the *phowa* practice of consciousness transference, and go to the pure land. So this is a very important part of this practice, and you should strive for this.

The Junior Tutor of His Holiness, Kyabje Trijang Dorjechang, gives an analogy. Imagine a Tibetan living in India under very poor circumstances. He has left his family back in Tibet, and they all—mother, father, relatives, a great household—are very wealthy there. The task of this Tibetan in India is to get back home, because as soon as he has made it back to Tibet, he will be welcomed into the arms of his family, and they will take care of everything. In a similar way, we are here in this world in a rather poor situation, and our task is to get back home, that is, to be with the Buddha in kechari and be under the direct guidance of Heruka and his consort.

Now having received the initiation of Vajrayogini, and having read these teachings, you are ready to practice. At the beginning, one doesn't think of oneself as tremendously fortunate, but if one tries on this perspective, and observes the lives of the people around one, then it slowly dawns on one that one does have an extremely rare opportunity right now. And one is particularly fortunate if one is able to have a Dharma relationship with His Holiness through receiving a teaching or an initiation from Him. This is something utterly rare and precious. I am not saying this because His Holiness is one of my gurus. It is much more than that. One can see His Holiness' behaviour who he is, what an extraordinary individual he is. Observing how he interacts with others, his compassion is simply manifest, clearly evident. As a monk he is unusually pure; he has a very strong inclination toward meditation. He is very earnest student and scholar; even now he studies the scriptures a great deal. When he gives teachings, they are enchanting. These erudite geshes are a pretty hard-headed lot. They are not easily impressed. So if someone comes along and gives teachings, they are going to sit back and reserve judgement.

They are not eager to accept or acknowledge another lama's perspective. When they listen, they listen carefully and discriminatingly. When they listen to His Holiness teach, these geshes are enchanted. They have a great reverence for His Holiness.

Retreat

It is also very good to do the retreat of this deity. The retreat called the serviceable (*las rung*) retreat is that which makes you fit to perform activities. Most people do not have a commitment to do the retreat, but it is quite wonderful to do it. If you can, it is good to practise the retreat, and do four hundred thousand of the three OM mantra, or if this is not possible, to do one hundred thousand of the mantra. Whichever, upon completing this number, you must then do ten percent of this number in addition, and then the same number of the wisdom-showering mantra. For instance, if you do four hundred thousand of three OM mantra, you then do another forty thousand of the three OM mantra and then forty thousand of the widom-showering mantra. The wisdom-showering mantra is not much different from the main mantra, you simply recite the three OM mantra up to PHAT PHAT PHAT SVAHA, and then add HUM HA ANTZE, so it becomes main mantra with these extra syllables at the end. After reciting this the proper number of times, you then do the fire puja at the end.[2] Having done so, you are authorised to engage in the various activities of Vajrayogini, such as the self-initiation.

Now for the retreat that you do, it will be quite sufficient to do the mantra one hundred thousand times. Upon completing the one hundred thousand, you do the wisdom-showering mantra, as explained above, ten thousand times. When you recite the three OM mantra, as you utter each mantra and move one bead, you should imagine a Vajrayogini merging into yourself, into your mind, and while reciting the wisdom-showering mantra, you should imagine countless emanations of Vajrayogini merging into yourself and blessing your mainstream.

If you do what is called the great '*nyen chen*' (བསྙེན་ཆེན་), then the greatest way of doing this is to offer this mantra one hundred times one hundred thousand times, that is, you recite the mantra ten million times. There is also the intermediate retreat, in which you offer thirty-two hundred thousand mantras. The great one of ten million takes about three years. One of my disciples has done this great retreat three times. Having finished the retreat three times, over nine years of practising, he came to me and said, 'Well, I'm not dead yet, I'm going to do two more'. So on the fifteenth of the next month he began his fourth great retreat. This man has given one of his eyes away. He has an incredibly pure mind, and he is living high up in the mountains in strict retreat. Every three years he finishes one retreat, and comes down to greet me. I met him some time ago in Bodh Gaya, and then he went off again into the mountains. This meditator has experienced many very clear auspicious sings of his being under the direct guidance of the guru and of the deity.

If possible, before entering the retreat you should receive the oral transmission on the sadhana you are going to do during the retreat. This is stated to be very important, in order to receive the blessing of the lama for your retreat practice.

Before engaging in the serviceable retreat which makes you fit to perform the activities of this deity, it is very beneficial to do some preliminary practices ('sngon 'gro), which include taking refuge, making prostrations, offering mandalas, reciting the hundred-syllable Vajrasattva mantra of purification and doing guru yoga. Of course it is best to do atleast one hundred thousand each times each, but if there is not time, then we still have to do these to some extent. You can do the short mandala offering with just one verse. It is very helpful to do these, as they eliminate obstacles which can arise during the course of the retreat.

You need to eliminate all your doubts and uncertainties before you go into the mountains and do a retreat. Otherwise, it becomes very awkward. If when you are in a long retreat high up in the mountains, you may have to write a letter to your lama 'What about this problem?', and then you have another problem, write another letter, and so forth. You may get into a lot of correspondence.

During the retreat you should practise the sadhana in the way that has been explained here, but you should never show the mudras to the people who do not have the initiation or who, although they have the initiation, do not have respect for the practice of this tantra.

With regard to the actual retreat itself, first of all it is important to have the proper location. If possible it should be a place with a very vast horizon, spacious, open and where you can look far into the distance. Secondly, it is very good to have a very beautiful view, for instance of snow mountains. Whether or not this is possible, you should conduct your retreat in a place where the environment itself is conducive to your health. Some regions are by their nature unhealthy, so you must choose a salutary place. This includes the availability of good food, fresh water, clean air and so forth. The place should not be an abode of evil spirits, one where there has been disharmony between spiritual practitioners, and also free from dangers of predatory animals. Last, if possible, it should be a place that has been blessed by previous holy mediatators having practised there.

As for the time of beginning the retreat, there are two auspicious times. One is on the twenty-fifth day of the eleventh lunar month, and the other is on the tenth day of the twelfth lunar month, as in the Tibetan calender. These dates will of course vary from year to year with respect to the solar calender used in the West. These dates are especially auspicious days for Chakrasamvara practice, dates which possess great blessings. Therefore, these would be the very best times to begin. If it is not possible to start on either of those two days, then the tenth or the twenty-fifth of any lunar month are also excellent days for the Chakrasamvara Vajrayogini practice.

The house where you are doing the retreat should first be cleaned and made very pleasant. If you are in a place where it is appropriate to do so, then you can clean the floor with the five nectars of the cow, which are urine, excrement, yoghurt, milk and butter. These can be mixed with water, and then the floor can be washed with these five substances. Whether or not this is practical for your situation at the moment, it is good to know that this practice exists. This has been done by meditators for many centuries. Next you bless your meditation place that you have thus cleansed and purified, with nectar pills, if you have them. Put the nectar pills into the inner offering while reciting the mantra OM AH HUM, in order to cleanse and purify the inner offering. Now, for the blessing of the inner offering, you are invoking the blessings of the Buddhas of the five families, requesting them to bless the five aggregates, which are represented by the five nectars and the five meats. Whereas in father tantras, such as the *Vajravarata*, the meats are in the cardinal directions and the nectars are in the intermediate directions, here, because Vajrayogini tantra emphasizes the clear light and cutting off self-grasping (*gcod*), the nectars are in the cardinal directions and the meats are in the intermediate directions. When blessed the five nectars and five meats, you should imagine that these are purified of all obstacles and faults, transformed into nectar of conjoined wisdom and bliss, and increased into a vast ocean of nectar.

Now, having prepared the food, as it were you have to invite the guests. You do this by doing the flaming mudra which invites dakas and dakinis. Visualise them appearing now in the space before you. Now with the sense offering mantras (OM VAJRA ARGHAM PRATICCHA HUM SVAHA, and so forth), you are actually making these offerings to the dakas and dakinis. Therefore, when you begin to recite each mantra, you snap your fingers outward at the level of your heart, to send forth offering dakinis who present these offerings to these invited guests. At the conclusion of each mantra, you snap your fingers again with your hands pointed towards your heart. In this way, you are drawing the offering dakinis back into your heart. You should have send them out either three times, or if you have time, seven times. This is an auspicious sign for the seven branches of Kha jor (embrace). (*or the "seven kisses of perfection*).

After blessing and offering the inner offering in this way, then sprinkle the inner offering while reciting the same mantra, to purify and bless your abode.[3] If you cannot obtain nectar pills, simply bless your inner offering with the mantra OM AH HUM, and then sprinkle the inner offering while reciting the mantra, to bless your abode.

If it is possible or convenient, in your meditation place, you should be facing the west. You should definitely have an altar with an image of Vajrayogini, whether it is a thangka or a photograph, or a statue. If it is too inconvenient to actually face the west, you can simply visualise that you are facing in this direction.

If you can find someone who knows how to do it, it is very good to have the three torma offerings. These are in the shape of the usual torma, ornamented with a four-petalled lotus. They are red in colour and have a variety of decorations, and are done in slightly different ways according to the tradition of various monasteries. The central principal torma is the offering to Vajrayogini herself, and then there is a slightly smaller one which is offered to the general dakinis, and this is placed to its right (your left). Apart from its size, it is in all other respects identical to the principal torma, being red and having the four-petalled lotus and so forth. Another torma placed to the right of the central torma is the offering to the Lord and Lady of the Charnel Grounds. They are the chief guardians of Vajrayogini and it is round at its base and then triangular at the top, with the three faces. Around its base are seven little stick-shaped pinches of dough—with indentions from being squeezed in your fist. All these tormas should be made out of clarified butter and tzampa. There is another torma called the *Og-min-ma* (Akanistha), which is offered to the protectors in general, who are led by the Tent Mahakala who resides in Akanistha, and others like the Lord and Lady of the Charnel Grounds, Palden Lhamo, etc. (*Traditionally it is coloured red*). And finally, there is a torma, also left uncoloured, to be offered to the local deity who is the lord of the site.

If possible, you should arrange four rows of the sense offerings, from *argham* (water for drinking) to *naividye* (food). These are offerings to the yidam (Vajrayogini), to the mundane deities, to the Dharma protectors and guardians, and to yourself generated as the deity. There is one row of offerings for each of those four. The three for the Vajrayogini generated in front, the mundane deities and the Dharma protectors and guardians are all arranged beginning from the deity's left (your right). The offering to yourself as the deity is arranged beginning from your left. Starting from the left is a special feature of the mother tantras, such as Vajrayogini. If it is not practical to make four rows, then it is all right to arrange only two rows, one for the front generation deity and one for the self-generation deity. Each of the rows of the sense offerings has a *naividye* or food offering, which doesn't need to be offered freshly each day: you can make an offering of a food which is not very perishable, such as tzampa, and keep that in a jar so that it lasts for the duration of the retreat. If you are not able to make the proper torma, you may simply set up five stacks of biscuits: (*more usually*) a central one for Vajrayogini, on to the left (from one's viewpoint) for the general dakinis, one to the right for the Lord and Lady of the Charnel grounds, and another two for the protectors (called "the Akanistha one") and the lord of the site.

Offering of alcohol and meat are indispensable. It is best not to put alcohol into the torma, as it would go stale. Rather, keep the alcohol offering in a bottle, and keep some dried meat in a container, so that it will stay there for the duration of the retreat. For highest yoga tantra, meat and alcohol are essential.

For your meditation seat, you should first draw an image of a swastika, with its points going clockwise. Upon this you place stalks of kusha grass, with their points facing inward, and then on top of these a kind of grass called durwa (*rtza ram pa*) with many joints. You can often find kusha grass in the West in Oreintal neighbourhoods, such as Indian or Chinese shopping areas, where kusha grass is sometimes sold in the form of brooms. The many-jointed durwa grass is for long life, and the kusha grass is to symbolise accumulating merit in order to increase concentration and mental clarity. The seat itself should be comfortable, with the back part slightly raised. You should have a wonderful seat, such that you can generate the confidence that just as the Buddha attained enligthenment when sitting on top of a similar seat of kusha grass and so forth, you yourself will be able to eradicate self-cherising and the misconceptions about the self, to eradicate the obstacles to liberation and to the full enligthenment, on this very seat.

You should also have a vajra, bell and damaru. If you can obtain a skull-cup it is also very good. If you don't, then you can keep the inner offering in a container with a lid. These implements—the vajra, bell, damaru and skull cup—are called the implements of commitment. Just as a very fragrant flower attracts bees from all around, so these implements of commitment attract the dakinis.

You must also have an assistant or helper for your retreat. This should be a good helper, who has a gentle mind full of respect and reverence for the practice, one who is clean and knows what has to be done, such as pulling the curtains at the appropriate time of day, and one who knows your wishes almost without your having to express them. This kind of helper is the best.

In generating the wheel of protection, you should visualise certain people within your wheel protection, which would include all of your lamas, even if some of them are in Tibet, so that there maybe no chance of meeting them during your retreat. You still place them inside your protection wheel as an auspicious sign. In your imagination you should also include a physician or healer, in case you become ill and have to meet with them. Also, if there are some friends who you must see during your retreats, perhaps four or five such people, you would place them also inside your protection wheel. Furthermore, during the retreat you shouldn't peek out the window to see people passing by, or anything that will divert your attention away from the practice. If you do, then the signs of the deity will vanish. In fact, for a very strict retreat, you don't even see the sky. The more properly you conduct the retreat, the greater will be the blessing. If you wish to make contact with some of these people you have included within your protection wheel, then if at all possible, it should be done by means of writing notes or letters. But if possible, do not meet the person.

On the very first day of the retreat clean the retreat place, sweeping up any dust and so forth from the ground and put aside the sweepings, which will be taken out later. Then you first make the *geg tor* offering, which is the offering for expelling hindering spirits and influences, and then take this outside. Next you make the *zhidag* torma offering, the offering to the local spirit called the lord of the site, and (*the sweepings are taken out with the geg tor*). For the first of these, making the *geg tor* offering, you first generate yourself as Vajrayogini, and maintain the divine confidence of being Vajrayogini. As Vajrayogini, you make this offering to all the local spirits in this region, and ask them for their aid in expelling all harmful influences, both animate and inanimate. Then while reciting the mantra of this offering, you visualise all the malignant spirits being banished so that they cannot return.

Next there is the *tsam tho* (མཚམས་མཐོ་ literally "boundary mar- ker"), which is not an offering, but a symbol to mark the boundary of your retreat place. You make a mound of earth, and place on top of this a piece of kusha grass wrapped in a white scarf called a *kha tag*, and you visualise this as Kandarohi (Tibetan *Dum kye-ma* དུམ་སྐྱེས་མ་), who is the protecting dakini (for this practice). You place this marker on the border of your retreat place at the point beyond which you will not go during your retreat. For instance, you could place this above your door. You imagine this dakini as being the guardian of the boundary, warding off any harmful influences that might arise from outside, and keeping any type of attainments that are generated during your retreat from going outside. Having generated this *sang tor* as Duchana, you make *bul tor* offerings to her and request her help for the duration of the retreat in warding off any kind of negative influence. Having offered this *bul tor*, you come back to your seat, if possible facing the west, but if not, then visualising that you are facing the west.

To begin your first meditation session, dip your left ring finger into the inner offering, and taste it on your tongue, while visualising that this experience of tasting it is purifying all your obscurations. This is called 'experiencing the nectar'. Then you purify your abode, dipping your finger into the inner offering again, and sprinkling a drop into each of the four directions, while reciting the mantra OM KHANDAROHI HUM HUM PHAT.

For the blessing of the seat, you visualise that on the crown of your head, the white syllable OM transforms into a white wheel marked with a syllable OM in its centre. At your throat the red syllable AH transforms into a lotus marked with a red AH at its centre. At your heart the blue syllable HUM transforms into a five-spoked vajra marked with HUM at its hub. Bless these three places by sprinkling each place in turn from the inner offering with your left ring finger. Then with the fingers of your left hand extended and your thumb folded in and holding vajra against your palm, touch your seat, and think that your seat has become in the nature of a vajra, being indestructible and immutable. While doing this, recite the mantra OM VAJRA HASANA HUM SVAHA. This practice is called blessing the seat. Throughout the retreat your meditation seat must not be moved. Also, you should not sleep on your seat. You should have a separate place for sleeping.

The above are the preparations for the retreat, and may be done either in the morning or in the afternoon. After completing these elimination of hindrances, blessings and so forth, then you can relax, have a cup of tea, and take it easy. It is not necessary for you to remain on your seat.

Then, after the sun has gone below the horizon, you should start your first session for the first day. You should not start while the sun is setting, but only after it has completely set. There are four times during each twenty-four hour period in which you should be having between-session breaks. These are sunrise, noon, sunset and midnight. Because these are times when there are naturally (*more precisely*) objects to single pointed concentration. It is advisable to schedule your meditation practice so that you are not meditating at any of these times. So now, after sunset begin your first session, and do the complete sadhana together with the auspicious verses. Recite the mantra as many times as you like, but do not count these mantras said in this session toward your full one hundred thousand, or however many you are accumulating.

As you sit down to begin this session, you should contemplate the preciousness of this life, its great significance, its rarity and fragility. Further, contemplate the rarity of hearing the Dharma, the rarity of meeting spiritual masters who are able to guide us in Dharma practice, and the rarity of being able to make use of these teachings and guidance to eliminate our beginningless faults and develop limitless virtues. When thinking of this, you can rejoice in this unparalleled opportunity. You should begin your session with great joy. It is stated in the Chakrasamvara tantra that even if you are in a very barbarous place where there is no Dharma, your meditating on Chakrasamvara or Vajrayogini attracts all the dakas and dakinis to your abode, just as a field of flowers attracts swarms of bees. By thus attracting these hosts of dakas and dakinis, the whole region and the people around are also blessed. Even the water in the area receives a special imprint which is beneficial for the minds of those who drink it. Through this practice it is possible to go the Akanistha pure land in this life. Even if this doesn't occur, at the point of death or in the bardo, dakas and dakinis holding victory banners will come to you and lead you to the Akanistha pure land.

The morning following your first session, you should get up at dawn; not a sunrise, but when the first light appears in the sky. In the summertime this is about three-thirty. You should do four sessions per day, doing the complete sadhana in the first session, and for the second and third leaving out some parts of the extensive sadhana. During the fourth session, do the complete sadhana again.

During the retreat it is very important to be somewhat relaxed at the beginning, not too strict or tense. Gradually you can increase the discipline of the practice, so that you are practising hardest in the middle of the retreat. Then it is also very important toward the end of the retreat to gradually loosen up, so that you are little relaxed at the end. Otherwise you can strain yourself by beginning the retreat with a feeling of pressure, or ending the retreat with too tight a discipline, and feeling let down when suddenly you are finished. It is important to increase and decrease your discipline gradually, so that you can start and finish the retreat with a feeling of joy.

An essential point to practice is that during the recitation of the mantra, you should sometimes do the complete visualisation and maintain the divine confidence of being the deity. However, most of the time you should practice analytical meditation on the essential points of the lam rim, such as impermanence, refuge, actions and their results and so forth. Mainly meditate on these, and now and again focus more on the visualisation.

The rosary you can use for this practice can be one of bodhi seeds (seeds from a bodhi tree), and this rosary can be used for any of the various activities of pacifying, increasing, magnetising or wrathful action. It is best if your rosary has one hundred and eleven beads, or if this is not possible, then one hundred and eight is also acceptable. If you can, it would be good to have the string of the rosary braided from nine strands by a virgin girl. There is a special way to bless the rosary, but you can do this in a very simple way by taking the rosary in both hands, and reciting the three OM mantra seven times. When reciting the mantra during the retreat, you should hold the rosary in your left hand, and begin each session of mantra recitation by each bead by hooking it with your (left) thumb and drawing it over your (left) ring finger. After doing seven or so mantra this way, then if that is too difficult, revert to using your thumb to draw each bead over your forefinger (i.e. the normal way to count) for the reset of the mantra recitation. Recite the mantra neither too quickly nor too slowly, neither so loudly that others could hear if they were present, nor so softly that you cannot hear yourself reciting. Recite each syllable distinctly and correctly. The Buddha himself gave these instructions for the way of reciting the mantra in the *Tantra Requested by Subahu*.

During the recitation of the mantra, when you are focusing on the visualisation of yourself as Vajrayogini, imagine that your body is being filled with the indefinite amount of red light being emanated and gathered back from the mantra and the BAM syllable. This purifies all of your unwholesome obscurations and their imprints. Sometimes do this visualisation, and at other times focus on the rays of light going out from the pores of your skin in all directions, reaching all sentient beings, purifying them of all obscurations and leading them to full enlightenment. This practice has a very profound meaning: in Tibetan this is called taking the fruit as the path (*'bras bu lam byed*). This means that the fruit or result of your spiritual practice is applied to your present practice, in that you are mentally creating a fascimile of a Buddha's body, environment, qualities and activities. Just as when someone attains the fully enligthened state of a Buddha, they send forth infinite rays of light, each of which provides many sentient beings with whatever it is that they need, in a similar way, although you are not actually Vajrayogini yet, you imagine being so, and engage in her Buddha activities by using intense visualisation. If you recite the mantra in conjunction with this meditation of taking the fruit as the path, each utterance of the mantra will be extremely effective in purifying your mindstream.

Some people begin a session sitting very upright, but in the course of the session they find that their head is nodding down more and more, so that they have only a nodding acquaintance with their meditation. If this kind of thing happens, you should clear your mind by contemplating this fully-endowed human life and impermanence. Doing this clarifies the mind, and also helps you feel like arising early in the morning. You will find it easy to get up early, and your mind will be clear. Of course you have to have some experience with this kind of contemplation, but if you practice this, then you will certainly achieve this result.

Concerning the contemplation on the preciousness of this human life and on impermanence, reflect on the life of Milarepa. Once his sister came to him, and of course he was naked, and she told him that this was very improper: 'You should have a sense of shame. Everyone will look at you, and think that you are very weird. You should have some clothing on.' So she gave him a piece of cloth and said, 'Sew this and make some clothing for yourself.' He agreed to this, and then, when he was starting to sew this cloth, he thought, if I die while making this piece of clothing, then I will have wasted some of this precious human existence. So he took the cloth and wrapped it over his finger to protect his mantras while he recited them. He felt such a sense of urgency that Dharma came before anything else. We can appreciate the power of his aspiration from reading his songs.

Looking also at the words of Geshe Potowa (*Po to ba*), he said that we are living right now as if we were already arhats. An arhat can be relaxed, because he has done what is to be done; his job is finished. And here we are, taking life easy, enjoying ourselves and feeling casual, as if we had already completed our task. Geshe Potowa states that when people like this meet death, suddenly there is panic. They tear their hair and grasp for breath; they meet the Lord of Death and it is like being tortured. So right now it is as if we are at a crossroads. Being at a crossroads in traffic, or being at a crossroads in your life, it is the same: it is a critical time, and the choice you make right now is going to make a big difference.

After reciting all the mantras, you offer the ritual fire offering of peace. Having done this, you are authorised to engage in the various activities including self-initiation, and to recite certain mantras to purify any faults incurred through not offering tsok on the tenth or twenty-fifth.

In order to make this practice one that can really transform your life, it must be accompanied by the attitudes of renunciation, of bodhicitta, and of a sincere, fervent aspiration to understand the nature of reality, as has been clearly taught by the Buddha. Without these attitudes, there will not be much benefit, whereas if you make the effort to cultivate these attitudes, and do your Vajrayogini practice in conjunction with this effort, then you will certainly experience the blessings of this practice; you, who are doing the practice, must have a Mahayana mind. In order to develop this, you should continually contemplate death and impermanence, refuge, the four noble truths and so forth, the stages of lam rim. You should cultivate loving kindness and compassion, realising that although we do not recognise other sentient beings as being our mothers from previous lives, nonetheless this is actually how it is. In fact, each living being has been the dearest person in the world to us countless times in the past. What harms these beings is suffering, and what benefits them is well-being, but even while desiring to avoid one and to gain the other, in their hapless bewilderment, people actually do what will bring them more suffering, and neglect to practice what will bring them joy. Thinking in this way is the method of developing loving kindness and compassion for all sentient beings. On the basis of this, you can train your mind in the cultivation of bodhicitta.

Then, having cultivated bodhicitta, you should seek and find a qualified vajra master. A qualified vajra master is one endowed with the ten outer and ten inner characteristics.[4] You should receive perfectly the tantric initiation from just such a master. Having done so, you should keep the vows and commitments as carefully as you guard your own eyes.

Then, meditate on both the gross and subtle levels of the stage of generation. Train your mind well in the stage of completion, involving the accomplishment of the illusory body, the clear light, and the great union. In this way, you will achieve the attainment of full enligthenment, in which all faults have been eradicated and all wholesome qualities have been brought to perfection. At this point, even one part of your consciousness is able to see conventional truth and ultimate truth simultaneously.

Before you can reach this completely perfect state of full enligthenment, you must have brought to fulfillment the stage of completion, for it is impossible to attain Buddhahood without having done so. Before you can achieve actual realisations of the completion stage, you must have brought to fulfillment the gross and subtle levels of the generation stage. And before the realisations of the gross and subtle levels of the generation stage can occur, you must have received initiation from a qualified vajra master. Without that, these realisation cannot occur. Before receiving such an initiation, you must have cultivated bodhicitta. Without bodhicitta, you are unable to receive the initiation. Before bodhicitta can arise, you must contemplate deeply the nature of sentient beings' situation in this cyclic existence, and how beings are unable to escape from suffering. Without realising this reality, bodhicitta cannot arise. This realisation of the pervasive nature of suffering, which is afflicting yourself and all others, cannot be achieved without contemplating the specific types of suffering such as that of impermanence and death, which presently holds us completely in its power. Such a realisation of cyclic existence as having the nature of impermanence and suffering does not come about without meditating on taking refuge and on the nature of cause and effect. This contemplation and realisation of these cannot occur without first devoting yourself to a qualified master. So every realisation on the path to enlightenment depends basically on your relationship to the spiritual master.

At this time we should be very careful to make good use of this special opportunity, and the potential of our present situation, and try to really see that we are living a human existence which is something far greater and has infinitely more potential than an animal's existence. If someone lives his or her entire life without any spiritual practice, then on the conclusion of that life, there is not the sligthest difference between such a person's death and the death of an animal. Even if you have no wealth at all, you can still maintain your life by going out and begin. But if you do not do any spiritual practice, then even if you have plenty of wealth and build yourself a huge house, your life still is not much different from that of a fortunate animal. The Buddha himself told his disciples that 'I am showing you the path to liberation and enlightenment, but it's up to you to put it into practice. You have to achieve this by yourself.'

Uncommon Inconceivable Yoga

These are the instructions for going to Akanistha pure land without having to leave your body behind. These special extraordinary instructions are to enable you to do this. This practice can be done at the end of a sadhana session. If you are in retreat, then you can do this practice between sessions.

First you take refuge, and then recite the verse, 'Once I have attained the state of a fully enlightened Buddha, I shall free all beings from the ocean of suffering of cyclic existence, and lead them all to the bliss of full enlightenment. It is for this purpose that I shall practise the stages of Vajrayogini's path.' Then you generate yourself as Vajrayogini with one face and two arms, and all the characteristics.

Then visualise the body of yourself as Vajrayogini as being hollow inside, clean and pure. Through the centre of your body, visualise the central channel, as thin as a straw, but as clear as glass. It is very straight without any bends. Visualise that it ends at your crown, and that it has an opening at that point. On the right side of the central channel is the roma channel (*rtza ro ma*), red in colour, which ends at the opening of the left nostril. On the left is kyangma channel (*rtza kyang ma*), white in colour, which ends at the opening of the left nostril. The lower ends of both the right and left channels are visualised as being slightly lower ends toward and almost meet the central channel at its lower tip, three or four finger-widths below the channels are close to the central channel, with only a few millimetres between the central channel and each of the side channels. The left and right channels are slightly smaller in diameter than the central channel, and are the size of a blade of grass.

Next you draw in the energy winds by inhaling through your nostrils, and also visualise you are drawing the energy winds in from your anus, bringing the winds inside and raising them up. The winds come down from your nostrils to your navel, and from your anus up to your navel.

Now, Vajrayogini is standing on the two side channels at the navel. She has no cushion at this time, but she is wearing her ornaments, the bone ornaments, fifty-skull necklace and five-skull crown ornament, cleaver and skull-cup and the khatvanga. She is in the nature of your own subtle body and subtle mind. You should understand that she is in the nature of your own mind, not that you are outside looking in at her, but that you are this Vajrayogini. You should have the divine confidence of being her at the navel.

Now, to exercise the channels and the mind, yourself as Vajrayogini at the navel emanates another Vajrayogini, who goes up through the right channel and emerges through the right nostril, and remains there on the tip of your nose. Meditate on this Vajrayogini on the nose. Now, this small Vajrayogini on the tip of the nose emanates light to the whole surrounding environment, so that everything transforms into the double tetrahedron which is the mansion of Vajrayogini. Then the rays shine forth again, and purify all sentient beings. You visualise that in this way they are all transformed into the state of Vajrayogini. Now visualise that the whole environment which has become the celestial double tetrahedral mandala of Vajrayogini dissolves into the sentient beings who have become Vajrayogini. Then they all dissolve into one another, and then dissolve into the small Vajrayogini at the tip of the nose of yourself as Vajrayogini.

Then breathe in through both nostrils, and inhale that Vajrayogini at the tip of the nose, which is now one entity with the Vajrayoginis of the environment and all sentient beings. Then this Vajrayogini descends through the left, kyangma, channel, purifying all stains and obscuration within that channel as she passes downward. Then she reaches the Vajrayogini at the navel and dissolves into her. Then you do the entire procedure as before two more times, drawing the energy winds inward from above and below, then visualising Vajrayogini standing on the left and right channels, emanating a small Vajrayogini who goes up through the right channels, emanating a small Vajrayogini who goes up through the right channel, and so forth, up to the small Vajrayogini coming down and merging again with the Vajrayogini on the left and right energy-channels at the navel. Do this entire procedure three times altogether. This practice is called exercising the powers of the channels.

Now, yourself as Vajrayogini has a small Vajrayogini at your navel, who emanates many rays of dazzling brilliant red light, which emerges from the pores of yourself as the larger Vajrayogini. You should visualise this light very clearly. The light is clear as crystal, and shines forth abundantly in all directions, illuminating brightly all of space. Also, the Vajrayogini at the navel in particular should be visualised very clearly.

Then this Vajrayogini at the navel, who is actually your own subtle mind and subtle body, has a strong desire to go to Vajrayogini's pure land, Akanistha. So you have this powerful desire to go to this pure land, and you can hear the sounds coming from there, of melodious singing, bells ringing and damarus resounding.

Now the double tetrahedral mandala and the cushion of lotus and sun dissolve into yourself into your lower torso, and your arms dissolve into your upper torso. At this point there is nothing outside because the entire environment and all sentient beings have previously been transformed into the mandala and Vajrayoginis respectively, and dissolved into the small Vajrayogini who has come back to your navel. Now you must have the very strong sense of your own mind being inside the small Vajrayogini at the navel, and hold the divine confidence of being that small Vajrayogini, not as if you are looking down at her or from somewhere else, but you actually are her.

Now your mind at the navel, this Vajrayogini, starts coming up through the central channel to your heart. The two side channels also roll up to the heart, accompanying the Vajrayogini who is rising up to the heart. Now all of the channels are dissolving into that small Vajrayogini.

Now the Vajrayogini comes up to the crown of the head, and as she rises, everything left, that is, the rest of your body, is dissolving into her. As everything completely dissolves into your own mind as this Vajrayogini, you arrive at the crown of the head.

Now you shoot up to Akanistha like a tiny shooting star. Once you are in the pure land, you imagine yourself getting smaller and smaller, and dissolving into emptiness, still remaining in Akanistha. Then you meditate on this emptiness.

Do this practice three, seven, or twenty-one times. You yourself are Vajrayogini with the three channels and a small Vajrayogini at your navel. Each time, you exercise the channels three times and do the complete process of going to Akanistha.

It is essential that after you have dissolved in the pure land, you don't fly back to earth like a bird. In other words, don't imagine yourself coming back. Each time you complete the practice, with yourself meditating on emptiness in Akanistha, simply start over again right here as yourself. Generate yourself as Vajrayogini, and then do the practice. It is *actually slightly harmful to imagine coming back down.* Simply start again.

After doing this practice the appropriate number of times, visualise yourself as Vajrayogini again, and don the armour, as explained above. Then say the mantra OM SUMBHA NI SUMBHA and so forth. Then engage in the yoga of daily activities, wearing your clothes, eating, all the things you have to do, and then you dedicate all of these activities by saying a prayer of dedication.

These are the instructions for going to Akanistha pure land without leaving your body behind. If you don't go in this life, then you may go at death or in the bardo. There should be no doubt in your mind that you will be led to that state. Even if you are one hundred years old at the time when you go to Akanistha pure land, there you will have the form of a sixteen-year-old. The life span there is limitless. Whatever you wish for there appears. Here we have to work for what we want, but there we can receive it from space, as it were. There Heruka with his consort is always present, and will give teachings to you. You can emanate countless bodies in many forms from Akanistha to other pure lands. There is no doubt that all the beings who dwell there will attain the state of Buddhahood of Vajrayogini in one lifetime.

These are the principal instructions on how to go to Akanistha without your mind parting from your body. Unlike the practice of consciousness transference which can shorten your life span, these teachings are a very excellent method, because they do not harm your life span. If you were to fill a thousand rooms with gold, these instructions would be far more precious. The benefits of these instructions are very stable. They will not wear out or get used up, nor are they useful only for this life. If you put these into practice, they will be precious to you in all lives. Each of us will die one day, and there is no need to be afraid if you have put this into practice. Pandit Parchen became ordained at the age of one hundred, and subsequently attained the state of Akanistha. I received these instructions myself from Kyabje Ling Dorjechang. There are many meditational deities that you could rely on, but not one is superior to Vajrayogini. You should cultivate this deity as well as you can.

Appendix I

I and all living beings as extensive as space, from this time forth until the attainment of the essence of enlightenment, go for refuge to the glorious sacred Gurus. We go for refuge to the fully enlightened Bhagavan Buddhas. We go for refuge to the sacred Dharma teachings. We go for refuge to the Sangha community of Arya noble ones. (3x)

I prostrate to and take refuge in the Gurus and the three Precious Gems, and request you to bless my mind-stream with waves of inspiring strength. (3x)

Once I have attained the state of a fully enlightened Buddha, I shall free all beings from the ocean of suffering of cyclic existence, and lead them all to the bliss of full enlightenment. It is for this purpose that I shall practice the stages of Vajrayogini's path. (3x)

In the space before me, on a jewelled throne surrounded by eight great lions, on a variegated lotus and moon, is my root guru in the form of Vira Vajradharma, with a red-coloured body, one face and two arms, with the right playing damaru that reverberates with the sound of bliss and voidness, and the left holding a skull-cup filled with nectar. His left elbow supports a khatvanga, and he sits with the six bone ornaments, he is vibrant in the prime of his youth. He becomes of an essence incorporating all the object of refuge.

I make requests to you, precious Guru, who are the essence of all the Buddhas of the three times. I request you to bless my mindstream with waves of inspiring strength. (3x)

My Guru melts into the form of red light, which enters me through the crown of my head. At my head. At my heart, from an E-E (ཨེ་ཨེ་) arises a red double triangle, inside of which from an AH (ཨཿ) comes a moon mandala. At the centre of the moon mandala is a red syllable BAM (བཾ་). Around the edge stands the mantra.

OM OM OM SARVA BUDDHA DAKINIYE VAJRA VARNAYE

ཨོཾ་ཨོཾ་ཨོཾ་སརྦ་བུདྡྷ་ཌཱ་ཀི་ནི་ཡེ་བཛྲ་བརྞཻ་ཡེ་

VAJRA VAIROCHANIYE HUM HUM HUM PHAT PHAT PHAT SVAHA

བཛྲ་རོ་ཙ་ཎི་ཡེ་ཧཱུྃ་ཧཱུྃ་ཧཱུྃ་ཕཊ་ཕཊ་ཕཊ་སྭཱ་ཧཱ།

Light radiates from the surrounding mantra, filling my body and purifying negativites, hindrances and sicknesses of body, speech and mind. My body becomes a ball of light. From this complete transformation, I arise in the bodily form of Vajrayogini, on a sun and moon cushion. With my outstretched right leg, I tread on the breasts of red Kalarati. With my bent left leg I treat on the back of black Bhairava, who is on his stomach with his head facing backward. My body is red in colour, with brilliance like the fire of the eon of destruction. I have one face, two arms and three eyes which look up toward Dakini-land. With my right hand, I hold downward-facing, outstretched cleaver marked with a vajra. With my left, I hold up in the air a skull-cup filled with blood, which I partake of with my upturned mouth. With my left shoulder, I support khatvanga marked with a vajra, from which hangs a damaru, bell and triple banner. My glistening black hair covers my back down to my waist. In the prime of my youth, my desirous nipples full and erect, I experience ever-enhancing bliss. I have five dried human skulls adorning my head and a long hanging necklace of fifty dried skulls. Naked, I am adorned with the five mudra ornaments, standing in the centre of a blazing fire of pristine awareness.

At my bodily places, between flesh and skin, arise moon mandalas. On these, at my navel is a red OM BAM (ཨོཾ་བཾ་) in the nature of Vajravarahi. At my heart is a blue HAM YAM (ཧཾ་ཡཾ་) in the nature of Yamani, at my throat a white HRIM MOM (ཧྲཱིཾ་མོཾ་) in the nature of Mohani, at my forehead a yellow HRIM HRIM (ཧྲཱིཾ་ཧྲཱིཾ་) in the nature of Sachalani, at my crown a green HUM HUM (ཧཱུྃ་ཧཱུྃ་) in the nature of Samtrasani, and at all my limbs a smoke coloured PHAT PHAT (ཕཊ་ཕཊ་) in the nature of Chandika.

From the mantra at my heart, light rays emanate, going out from the pores of my skin, embracing all sentient beings of the six classes, and cleansing them of their unwholesome karma and obstacles, together with their instincts, and transforming them all into the bodily form of Vajrayogini.

PHEM! Light rays emanate from the syllable BAM at my heart and invite from Akanistha Buddha-field Vajrayogini encircled by all the yoginis and heroes of the ten directions, and also all sentient beings who have become Yoginis. They dissolve into myself. JAH HUM BAM HOH.

OM YOGA SHUDDHA SAVA DHARMA YOGA SHUDDHO HAM. (I am the nature of the yoga of the purity of all phenomena.)

Inside the double triangle at my heart is a moon mandala, in the centre of which is a syllable BAM encircled with a red mantra rosary, arranged counterclockwise. From these, immeasurable rays of red light emanate, cleansing sentient beings of their unwholesome karma and obstacles and making offerings to all the Buddhas. They bring back the potential and force of their blessings in the form of rays of red light which dissolve into the syllable BAM together with the mantra rosary, thus blessing my mindstream with waves of inspiring strength.

OM OM OM SARVA BUDDHA DAKINIYE VAJRA VARNANIYE VAJRA VAIROCHANIYE HUM HUM HUM PHAT PHAT PHAT SVAHA

(Recite the required number of mantra here)

Light rays emanate from the syllable BAM together with the mantra rosary at my heart and pervade all the three realms. The formless realm dissolves into the upper part of my body in the form of rays of blue light, the form realm dissolves into the middle part of my body in the form of rays of red light, and the desire realm dissolves into the lower part of my body in the form of white light. I, as well, melt into light in stages from above and below, and dissolve into the phenomena source. That dissolves into the moon, and that dissolves into the mantra rosary. That dissolves into the syllable BAM, and that dissolves into the head of the BAM. That in turn dissolves into the crescent moon (*da che*), and that dissolves into the drop (*tig le*). That dissolves into the squiggle (*nada*) and that as well, growing smaller and smaller dissolves into clear light emptiness.

From the state of emptiness, instantaneously I arise as the Venerable Vajrayogini.

At my bodily places, between flesh and skin, arise moon mandalas. On these, at my navel is a red OM BAM (ཨོཾ་བཾ་) in the nature of Vajravarahi. At my heart is a blue HAM YAM (ཧཱུཾ་ཡཾ་) in the nature of Yamani, at my throat a white HRIM MOM (ཧྲཱིཾ་མོཾ་) in the nature of Mohani, at my forehead a yellow HRIM HRIM (ཧྲཱིཾ་ཧྲཱིཾ་) in the nature of Sachalani, at my crown a green HUM HUM (ཧཱུཾ་ཧཱུཾ་) in the nature of Samtrasani, and at all my limbs a smoke-coloured PHAT PHAT (ཕཊ་ཕཊ་) in the nature of Chandika.

OM SUMBHA NI SUMBHA HUM HUM PHAT. OM GRIHNA GRIHNA HUM HUM PHAT. OM GRIHNA-

PAYA GRIHNA-PAYA HUM HUM PHAT. OM ANAYA HO BHAGAVAN VAJRA HUM PHAT. (2X)

By the merit of this may I quickly achieve the Dakini powerful attainment, and may I lead all beings, without exception, to this state. By remembering this one (Vajrayogini), sufferings of the heart are eliminated. If one meditates with perseverance, in this life the great mudra will be easily bestowed. May all be auspicious for achieving the supreme and mundane attainments of the ruler of Khachö.

Appendix II

Prayer to Vajrayogini

There is a brief mention of the uncommon inconceivable yoga in the prayer book published (in Tibetan) by the Tibetan Government Cultural Printing Press in Dharamsala. The four lines of this prayer speak of Vajrayogini, here referred to as Varahi, coming through the central channel and emerging through the crown of the head, and about the blood-drinking hero, who is Heruka with his consort. This prayer is on page 514. The translation here is by Alexander Berzin.

> When the inner Varahi has destroyed the creeping vine
> Of my preconceptions about grasping consciousness and the objects it grasps,
> And the dancing lady residing in my supreme central channel
> Emerges from my aperture of Brahma into the sphere of the pathway of clouds,
> May I embrace and sport with the Vira-hero Drinker of Blood.
>
> *nang gi phas mos gzung 'dzin 'khri shing bcom*
> *mchog gi dbu tir zhugs pa'i gar mkhan ma*
> *tsangs pa'i sgo nas sprin lam dbyings su thon*
> *khrag 'thung dpa' bor 'khyud cing rol bar shog*

❖

Notes

1. 'Dakinis of the three abodes"; there are two interpretations of this: one is that these are dakinis dwelling in the sky, on the earth, and below the surface of the earth; the other is that these are dakinis of the twenty-four sacred places on the earth ('born from fields',) mudras with realisation of the generation stage or the first stages often completion stage, and the mudras with the realisations of the Union That Needs Learning or the Union of No More Learning.

2. For the procedures of the fire puja of Vajrayogini, see *Guide to Dakini Land*, by Kelsang Gyatso, London: Tharpa Publications, 1991, as well as *A Manual of Ritual Fire Offerings*, by Sharpa Tulku and Michael Perrott, Dharamsala: LTWA, 1987

3. Nectar pills, as well as the five nectars of the cow can be obtained in pill form from the Gyuto Upper Tantric College or from Namgyal Monastery in Dharamsala, India.

4. For the ten outer and ten inner characteristics of a vajra master (*rdo rje slob dpon, vajracarya*), Tsong Khapa, in his commentary on Ashvaghosa's *Fifty Verses of Guru Devotion* (*Gurupancasika*, Toh. 3721), called the *Motivation of an Aspiring Disciple* (*slob ma'i re ba kun slong*, Toh. 5269; f.7b3-8b2), lists the ten outer characteristics as being skilled in: (1) drawing the mandala; (2) meditative absorption; (3) the mudras (4) the stances; (5) the seated postures; (6) recitation; (7) ritual fire offering; (8) devotion; (9) preliminary rituals and (10) concluding rituals. Also listed are the ten inner characteristics as skill in: (1,2) the rites of the two reversals (*phyi zlog pa*) [practices such as reversal through contemplation of the ten wrathful deities, and practices such as binding, after inviting the wisdom deities]; (3,4) the secret and wisdom initiations; (5) the practice of dissolving the union; (6) making the dedicated food offering (*bali*), such as the offering for the fifteen directional protectors; (7) vajra recitation; (8) accomplishing the wrathful activities; (9) consecration and (10) accomplishing the activities of the mandala. Tsong Khapa explains that the ten outer qualities are most important

chiefly in the three lower classes of tantra. The ten inner qualities are stressed in the Highest Yoga tantra.

In many tantras and commentarial texts by Indian and Tibetan masters, the personal qualities which a vajra master must possess are highly stressed. For instance, in his extensive commentary on the generation stage of the Thirteen Deity Vajrabhairava called *Jewel Treasure House of the Three Bodies* (tr. by Sharpa Tulku with Richard Guard, New Delhi: Tibet House, in press), Lhun-grub Paṇḍita explains in detail those qualities stated by Ashvaghosa to be indispensable to one who bestows initiation, namely being disciple in (physical) behaviour; (2) disciplined in speech; (3) intelligent; (4) forbearing; (5) just; (6) without deceit; (7) skilled in the practice of mantra and tantra; (8) compassionate; (9) learned in the explanatory texts; (10) experienced in the ten (outer and inner) categories (as listed above); (11) expert in drawing the mandala; (12) able to explain the mantras; (13) devoted and (14) in command of his senses.

Bibliography

Note: 'P' refers to the catalogue and index of the Peking Edition of the Tibetan Tripitaka (Tokyo: Suzuki Research Foundation, 1971); 'Toh.' refers to the Complete Catalog of the Tibetan Buddhist Canons (bka' 'gyur and bstan 'gyur) (Sendai, Japan: Tohoku Imperial University, 1934).

Arisal of Heruka
dpal khrag 'thung mngon par 'byung ba
'he ru ka mngon 'byung', 'chog-thug-gyi-gyu'
Shri-Herukabhyudaya-nama
Tr. Advayavajra, chings yon tan 'bar
P21, Vol. 2; Toh. 374

Ashvaghoṣa (rta dbyangs, 1st c.)
Fifty Verses of Guru Devotion
bla ma lnga bcu pa
Guru-pancasika
Tr. Padmākaravarma, rin chen bzang po
P4544, Vol. 81; Toh. 3721
English Translation published by LTWA, Dharamsala, India.

Lesser Samvara Tantra (Root Tantra of *Heruka Cakrasaṃvara*)
rgyud kyi rgyal po dpal bde mchog nyung ngu zhes bya ba
Tantrarajasrilaghusambaranama
P16, Vol. 2; Toh. 368

Tsong Khapa (blo bzang grags pa, 1357-1419)
Motivation of an Aspiring Disciple
slop ma'i re ba kun slong
Toh. 5269; f.7b3-8b2

*Samvarodaya Tantra (*Explanatory Tantra of *Heruka Cakrasamvara)*
dpal bde mchog 'byung ba zhes bya ba'i rgyud kyi rgyal po chen po
'sdom pa 'byung ba'i rgyud kyi rgyal po chen po', 'sdom 'byung'
Shri-Mahasamvarodaya-tantraraja-nama

Tr. gzhan la phan pa mtha' yas, sme lam grags
Rev. gzhon nu dpal
P20, Vol. 2; Toh. 373

Short Book of Devotional Recitation of Guru Yoga and Self-generation
bla ma'i rnal 'byor dang yi dam khag gi bdag bskyed sogs zhal 'don gches btus bzhugs
Dharamsala: Tibetan Cultural Printing Press, 1990 (tenth edition)

Tantra Requested by Subahu
'phags pa dpung bzang gis zhus pa zhes bya ba'i rgyud
Arya-subahuparipricchanamatamtra
P428, Vol. 9; Toh. 805